NAKED HOLLYWOOD

NAKED HOLLYWOOD

by
Weegee & Mel Harris

A DA CAPO PAPERBACK

Library of Congress Cataloging in Publication Data

Fellig, Arthur, 1900-1968.
  Naked Hollywood.

  (A Da Capo paperback)
  Reprint of the ed. published by Farrar, Straus &
Giroux, New York.
  1. Moving-pictures—United States—Pictorial
works. I. Harris, Mel, joint author. II. Title.
PN1993.5.U65F4 1976   791.43'0973   76-6050
ISBN 0-306-80047-0

ISBN 0-306-80047-0

First Paperback Printing 1976

This Da Capo Paperback edition of *Naked Hollywood* is an
unabridged republication of the first edition
published in New York in 1953. It is reprinted with the
permission of Farrar, Straus & Giroux, Inc.

Published by Da Capo Press, Inc.
A Subsidiary of Plenum Publishing Corporation
227 West 17th Street, New York, N.Y. 10011

NAKED HOLLYWOOD

CONTENTS

_____

FOREWORD

_____

IT TOOK OVER TWO HUNDRED YEARS for Lilliput to become a legend. In little more than two generations Hollywood accomplished a similar feat.

Lilliput, with the help of one author and one book, is a clearly defined place. Hollywood, despite thousands of chroniclers and millions of words, enjoys the clarity and definition of a morning mist.

Like any mistress it is either loved or hated. This tends to distort one's perspective and, in turn, the subject. There are more misconceptions haunting Hollywood than there are stars.

This little book attempts to exorcise those misconceptions. It has always been felt that the camera infallibly mirrored reality. Inevitably then, the word corroborated by the picture must impart to this book the rare quality of presenting the facts as they are— simply, honestly and objectively.

We regret that it has failed.

Mel Harris
1953

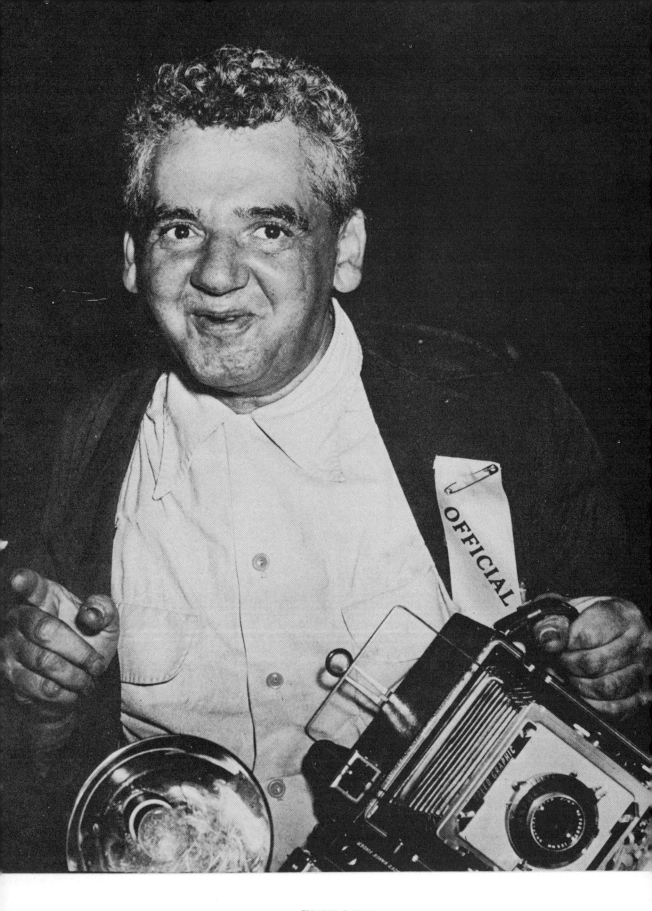

WEEGEE

MEL HARRIS

THE STUDIO is devoted to the mass production of illusions.

Today it consumes the talents of an army of kings, horses, and men.

At one time, the main tools necessary for picture-making were a megaphone, a strong cranking arm, and a plot.

Only the last has resisted change.

Act I   *DREAM FACTORY*

PEARLY GATES

St. Peter

De Lawd

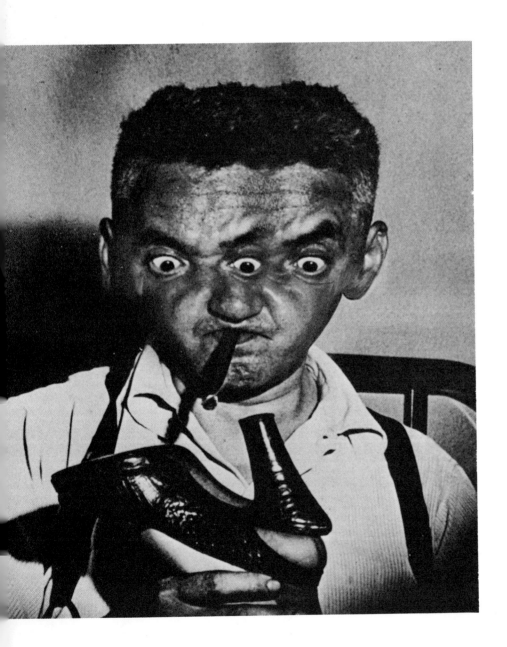

Talent scout

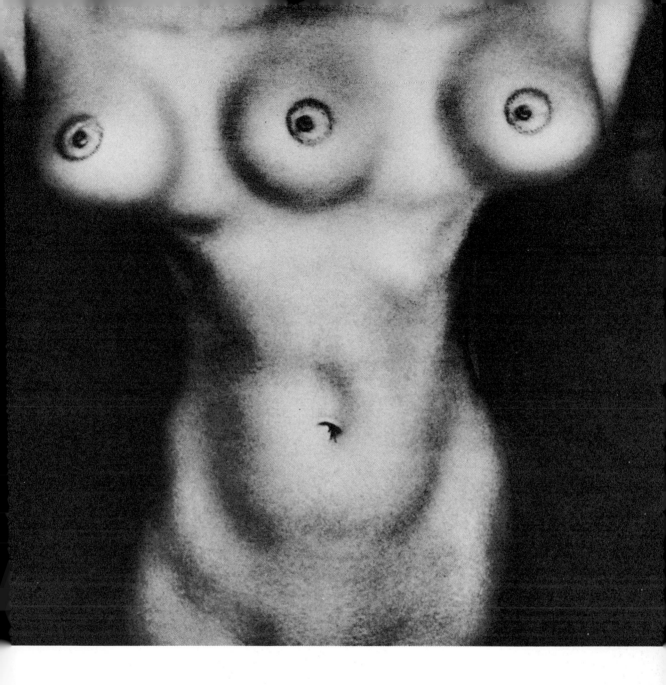

Talent

Story conference

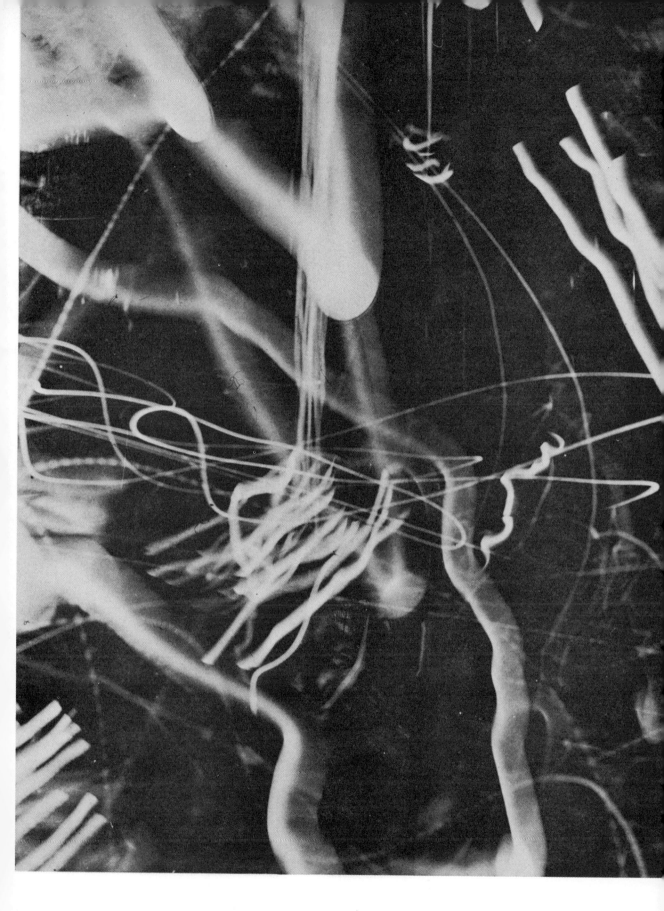

Story

Boy meets girl

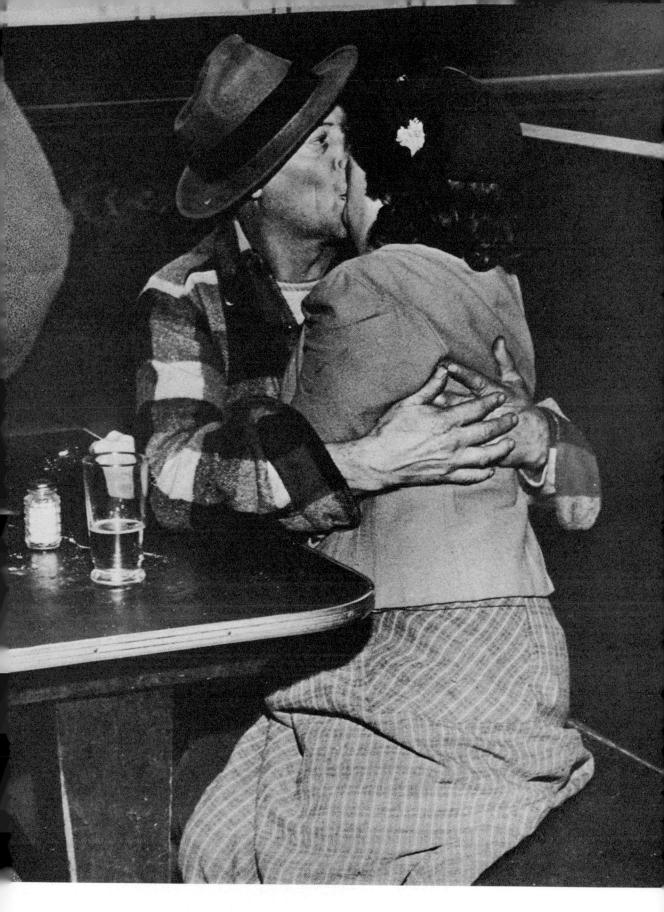

. . . boy gets girl

. . . boy loses girl

...HAPPY ENDING

Makeup dept.

Wardrobe dept.

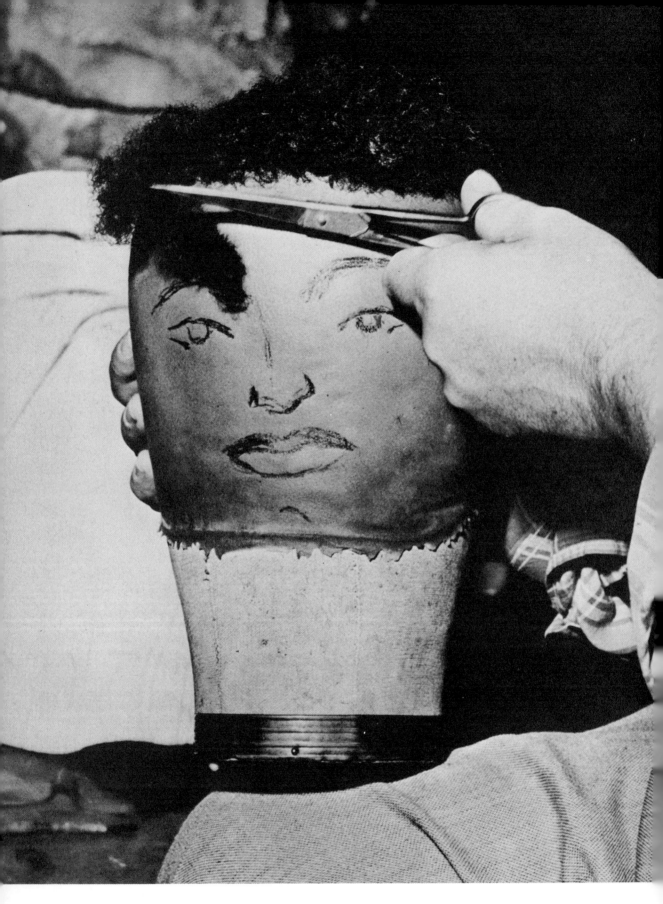

Personal hairdo

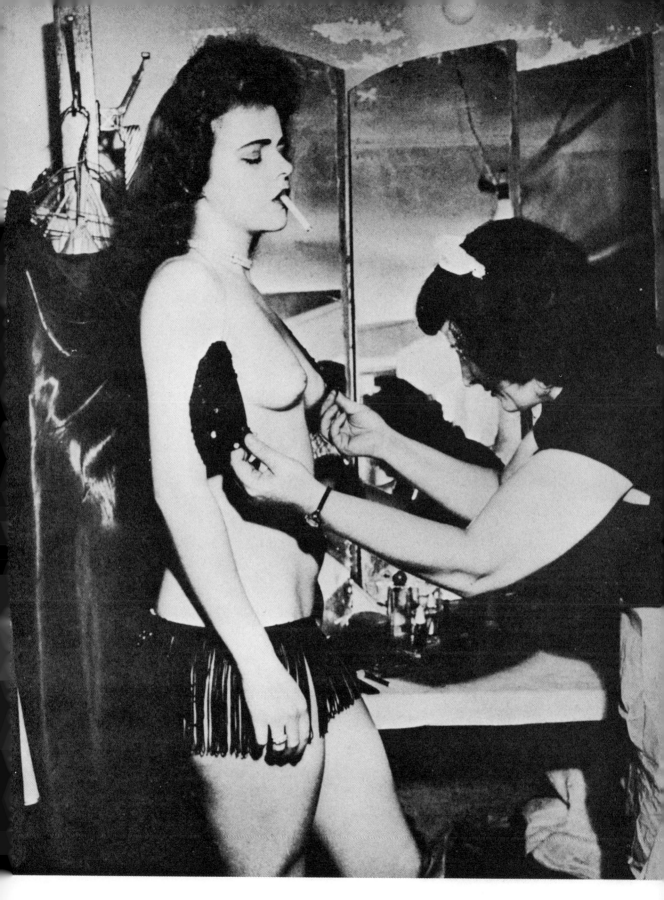

Personal maid

Hero

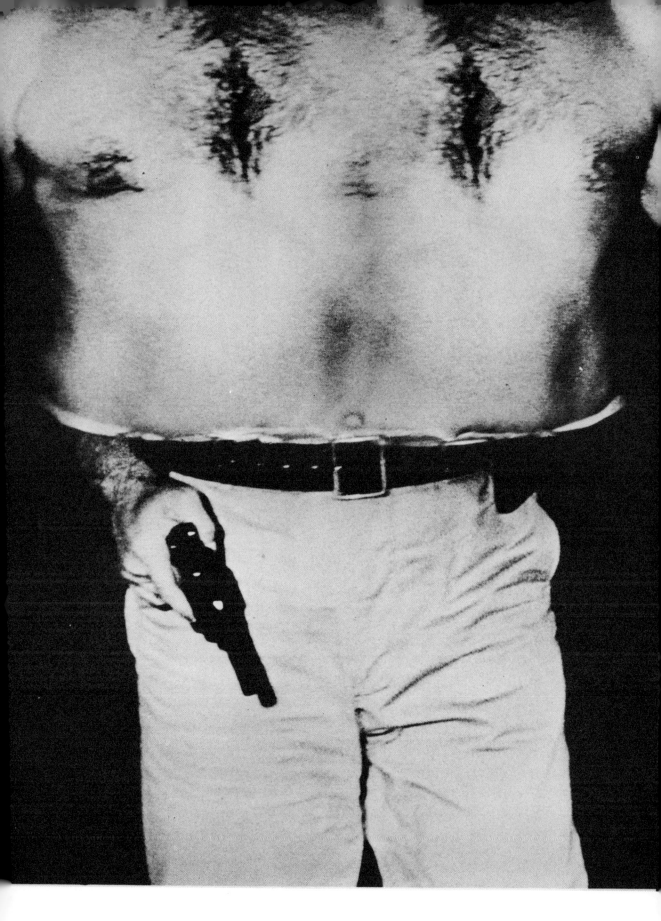

. . . villain

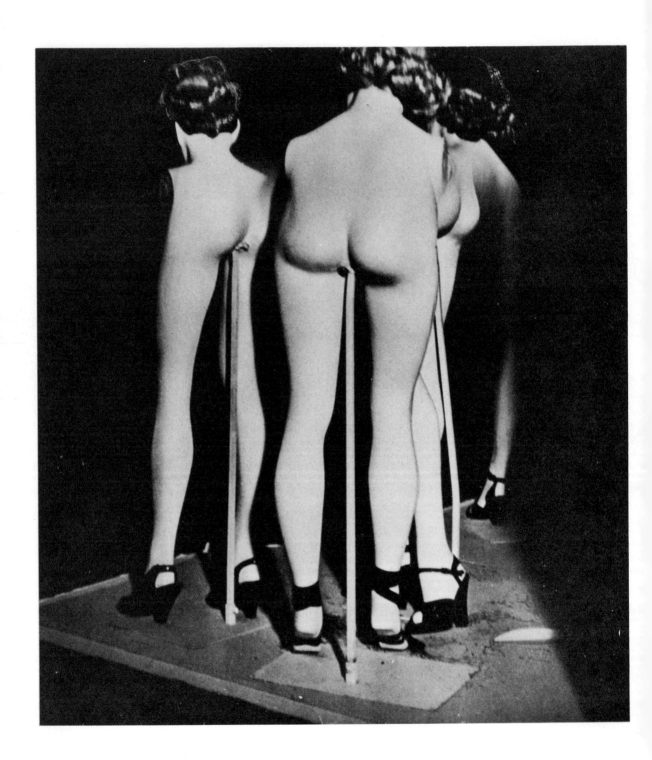

. . . bit players

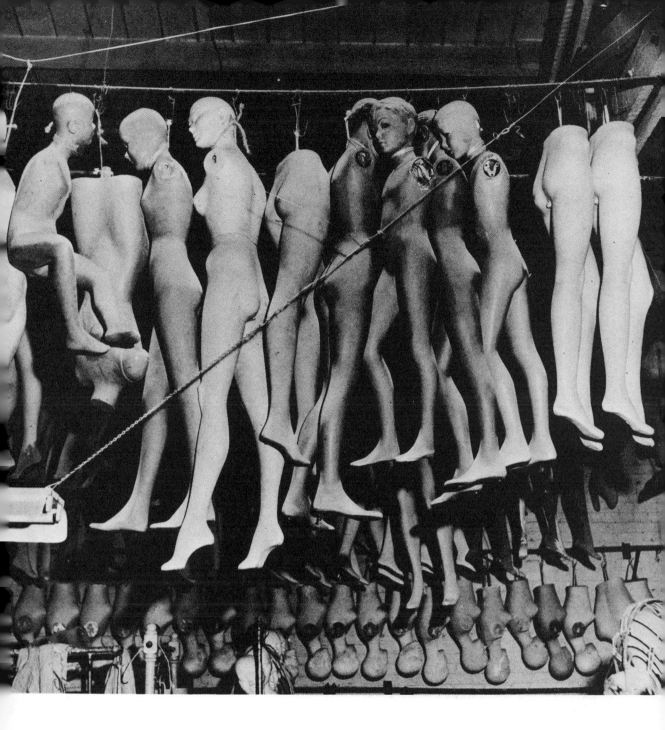

. . . extras

Trick rider

Stunt girl

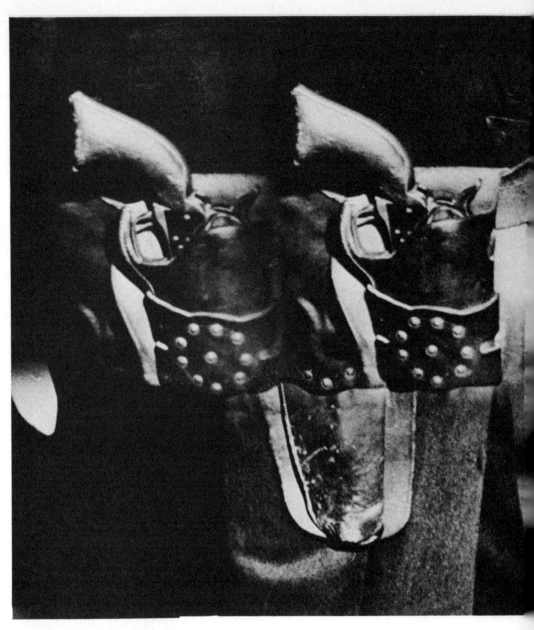

MUSICAL

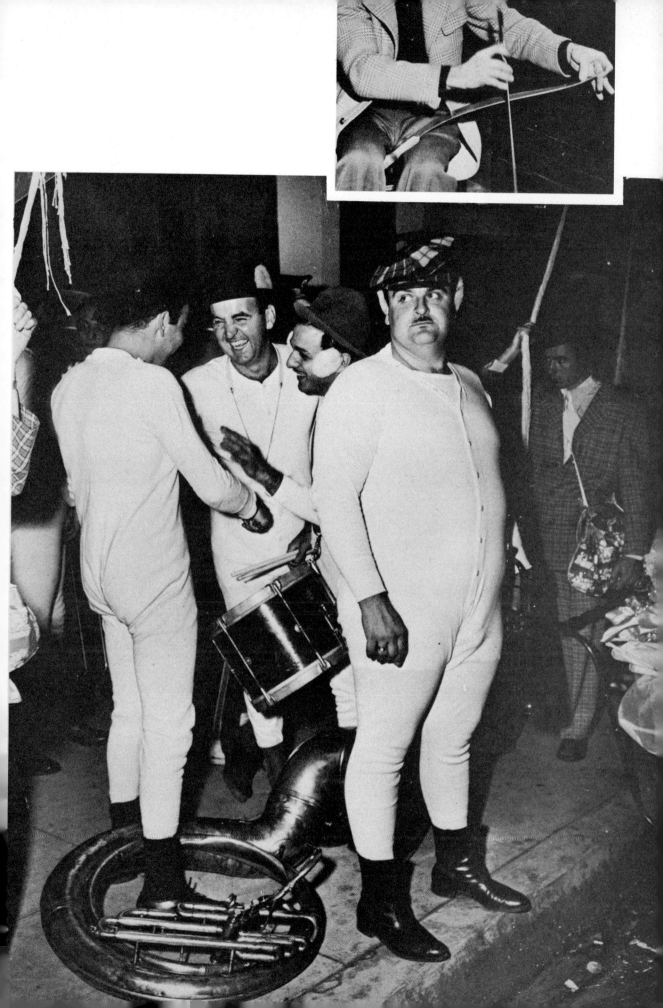

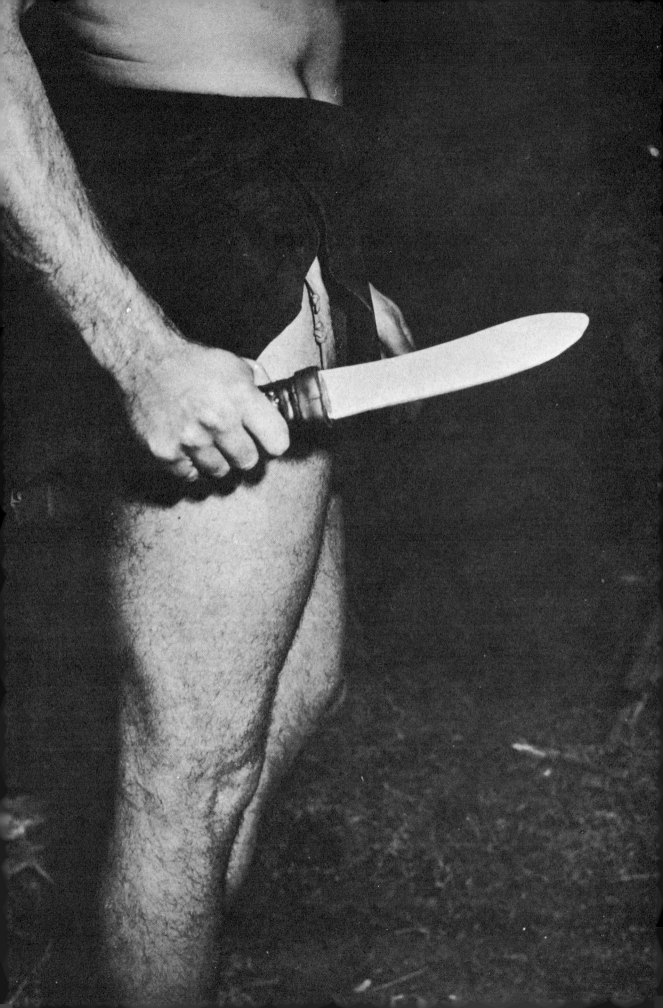

JUNGLE DRAMA

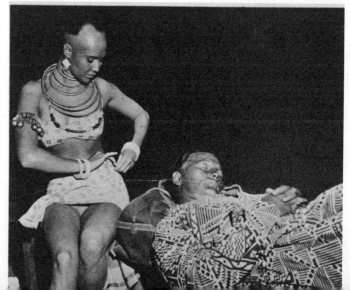

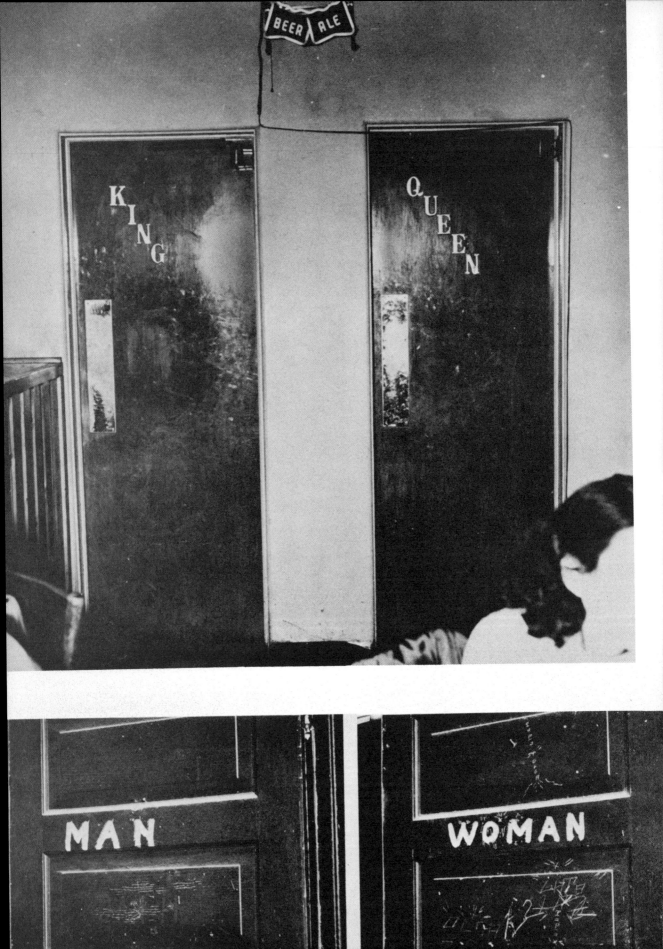

DOCUMENTARY

Roll 'em

M-m-m

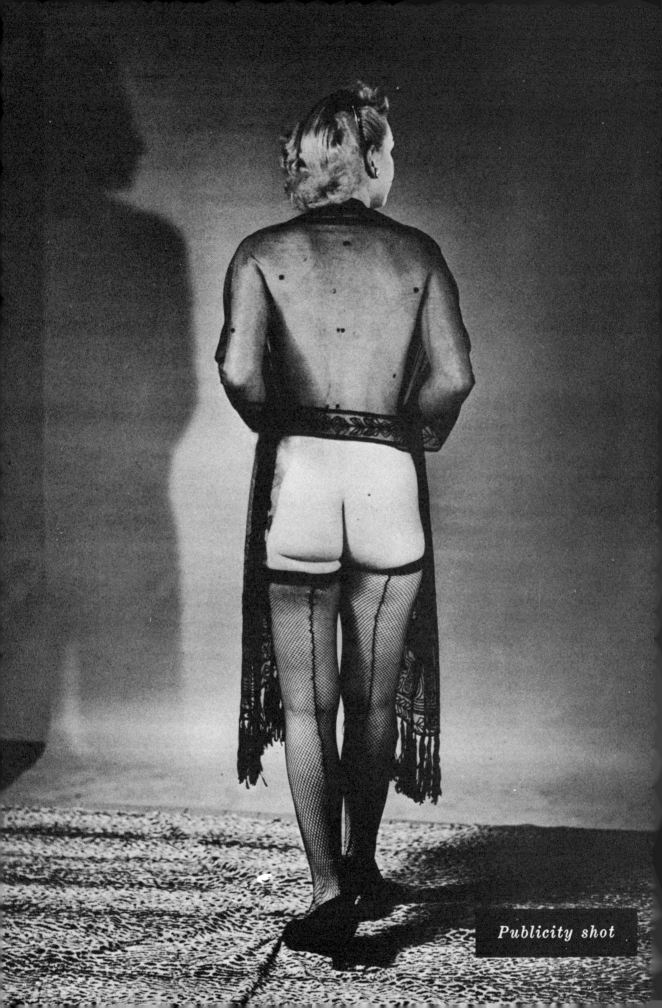

Publicity shot

Press agent

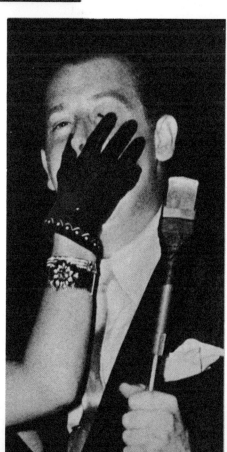

Censorship

OCCASIONALLY, THE STREETS OF HOLLY-
WOOD become the setting for a cherished
native ritual — the Hollywood Première.

The Première is a carefully prepared,
spontaneous display of affection between
stars and audience. Except for a new picture, in whose honor the shindig is given,
there is little variation. The stars come,
are seen, sign, and scamper.

Sometimes the guest of honor, the picture, is lost in the shuffle.

RIGHT LANE FOR PREMIERE ONLY

Act II   THE PEOPLE

THE STARS LOOK DOWN

Everyone enjoys the show

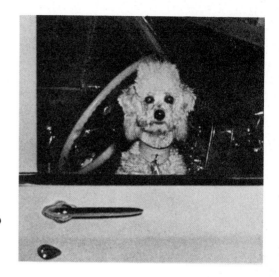

...me too

...not me

Rain or shine

. . . the stars come out

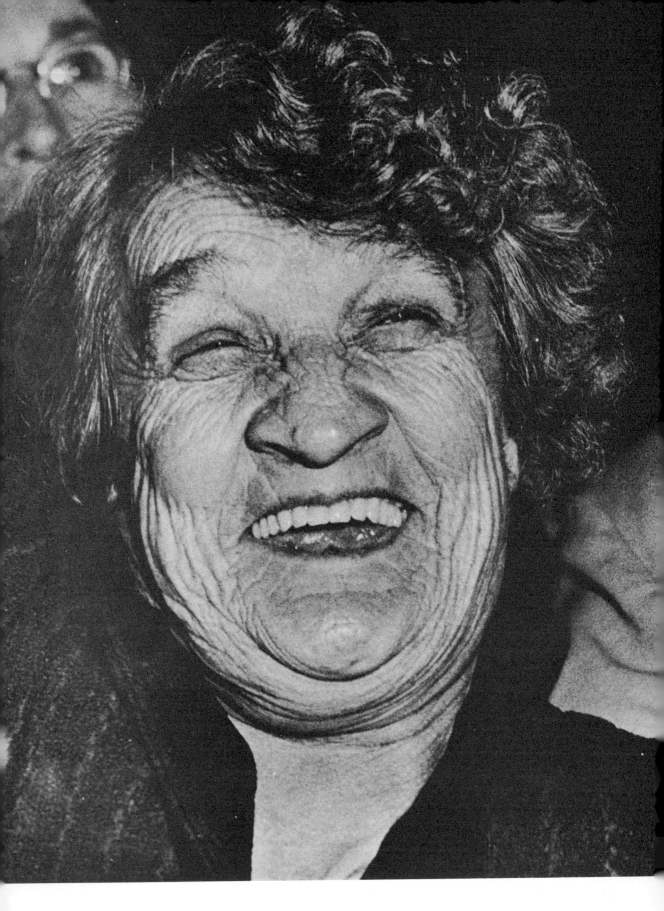

Never too old

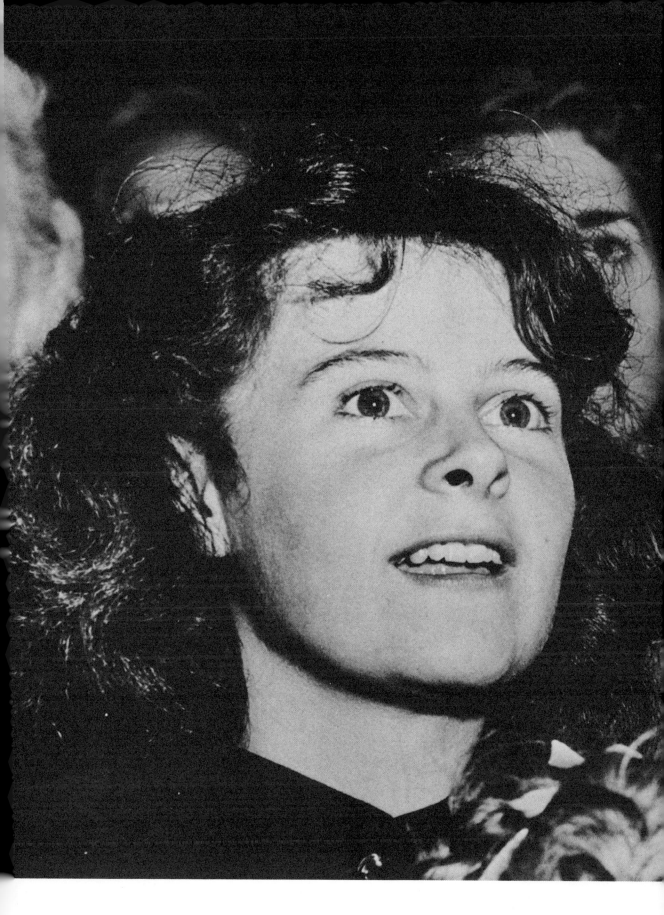

...or

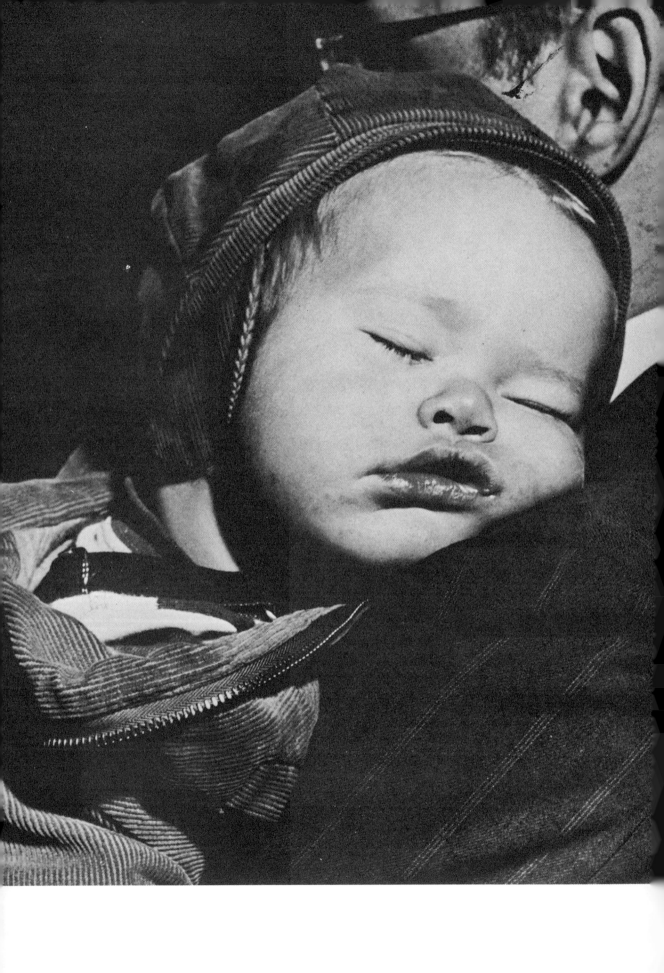

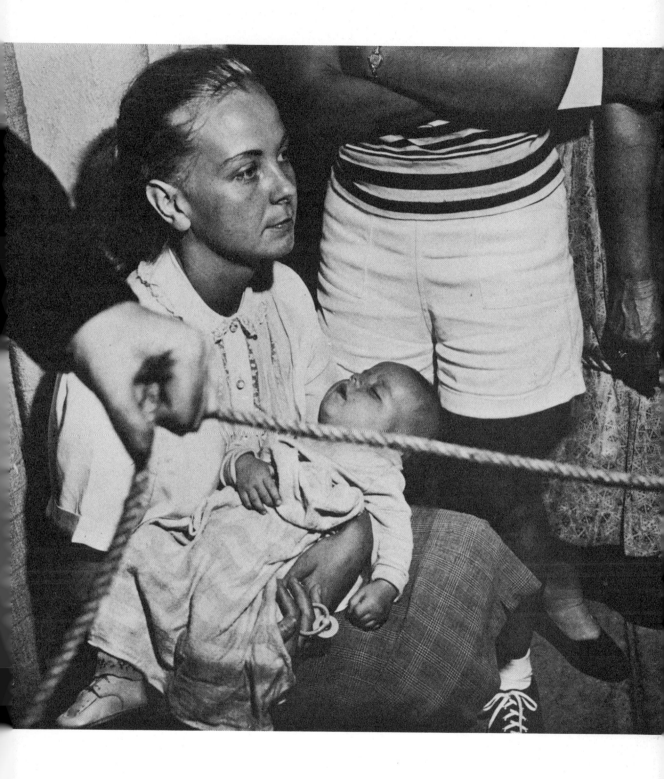

...too young

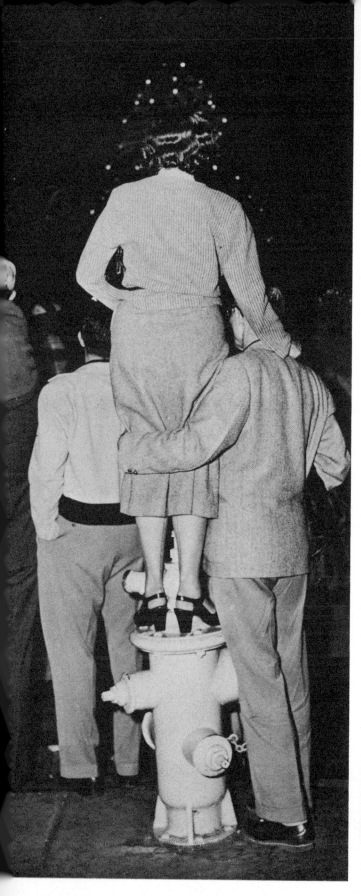
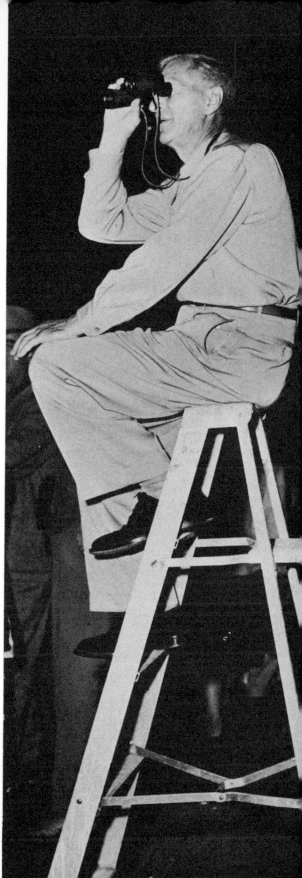

FIRST ROW BALCONY

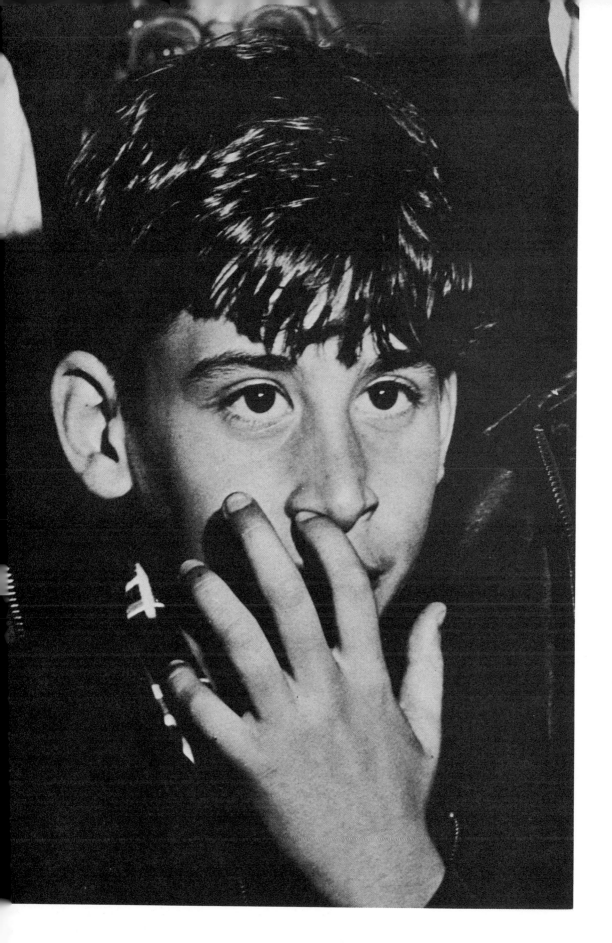

The moving finger

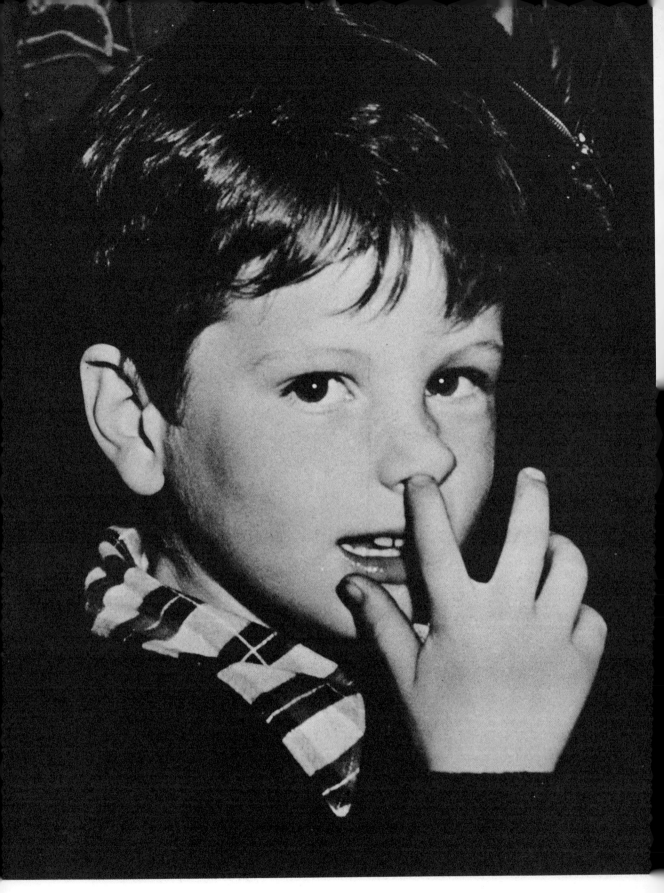

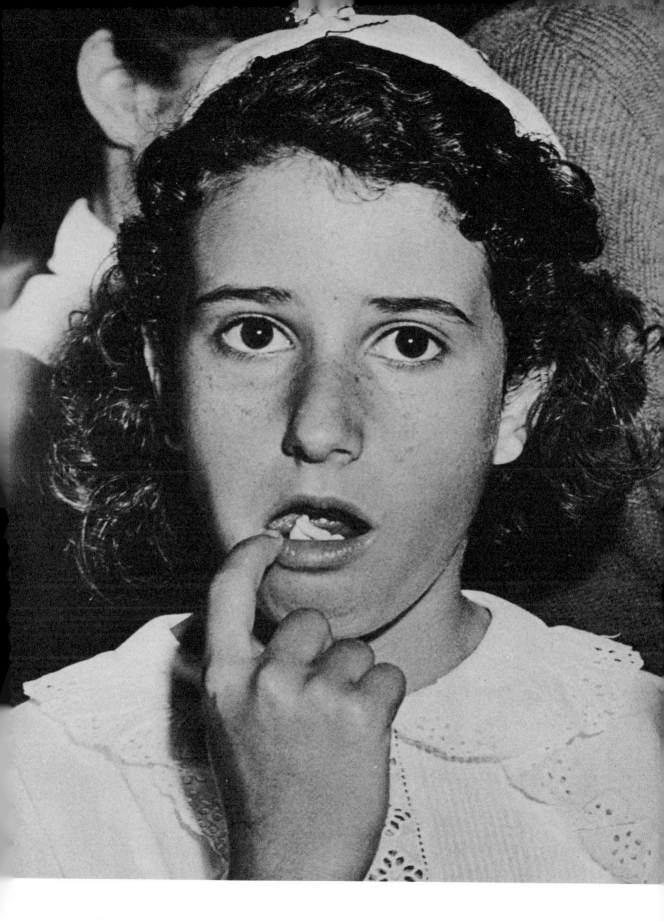

...moves on

Fire torpedo one

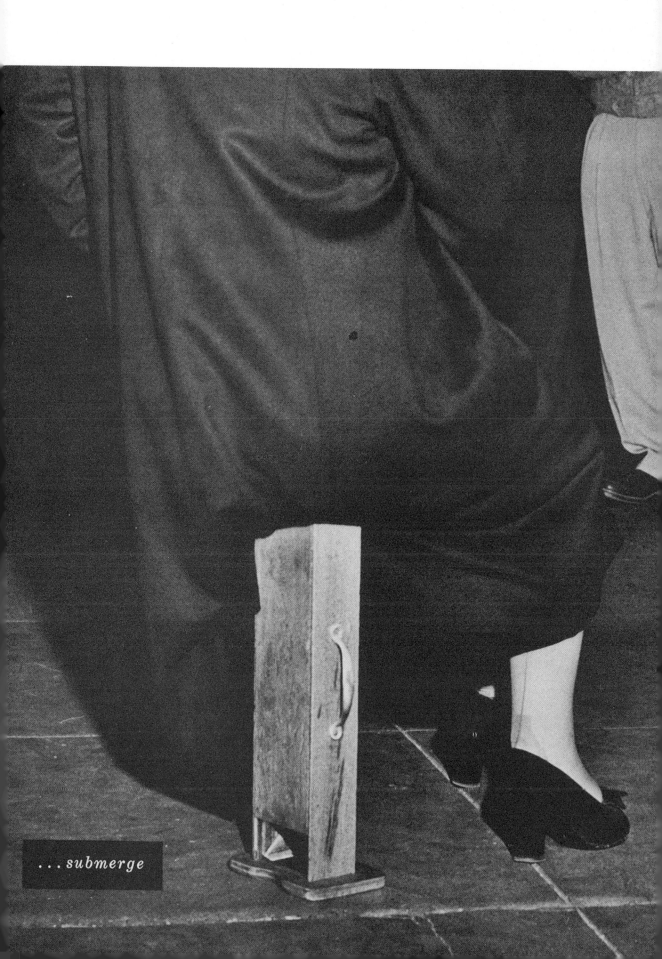

. . . submerge

Bible

Hoppy's happy

. . . Norma, too

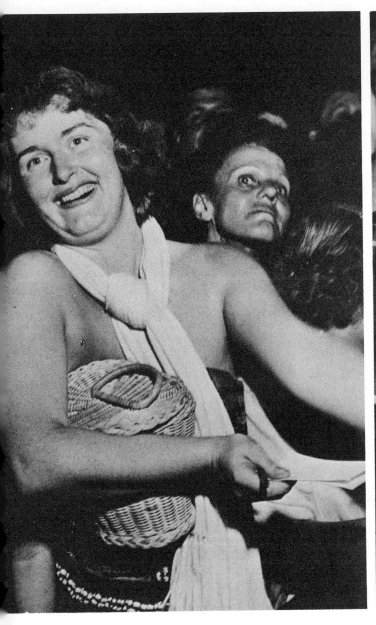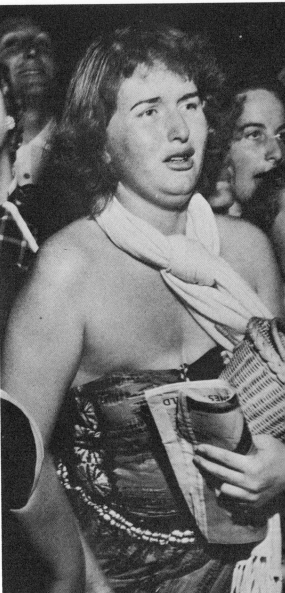

AN AMERICAN TRAGEDY: no autograph

A STAR'S PRIVATE LIFE is a matter of public concern.

To insure this, the imagination of the press agent is often taxed, but, fortunately, never exhausted. He depicts his client as a sophisticated, man-eating *femme fatale* in pin-curls, devotedly stirring a potful of Pablum.

Publicity stories are intended to intrigue the fans, and, to add to the feeling of realism, they are presented as "news".

Often they are news to the stars themselves.

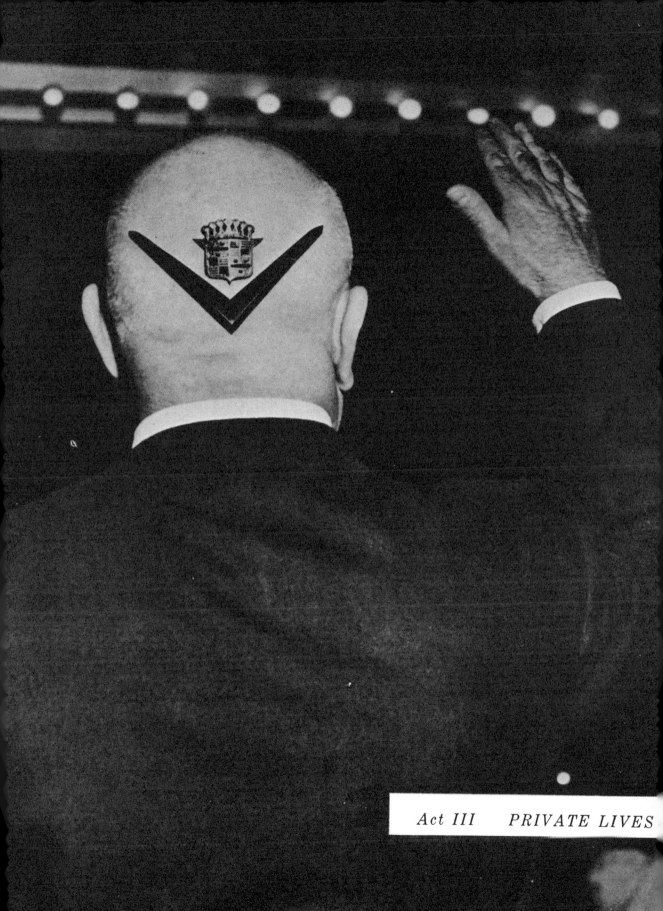

Act III   *PRIVATE LIVES*

STANDARD EQUIPMENT

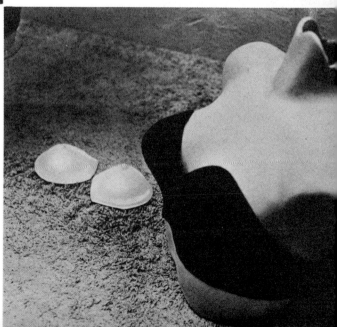

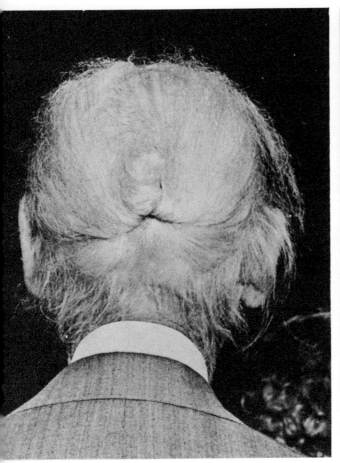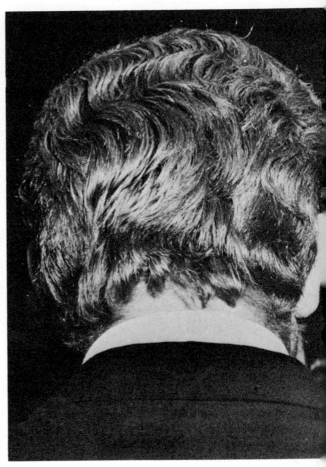

Silent star   *Kirk*

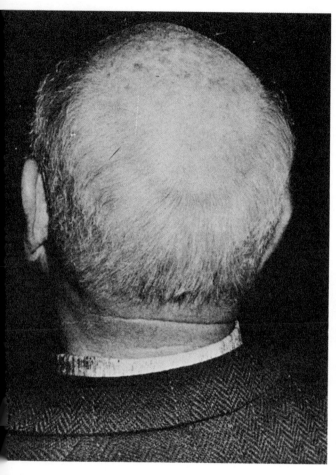 

Cecil   *Ann*

GONE WITH THE WIND

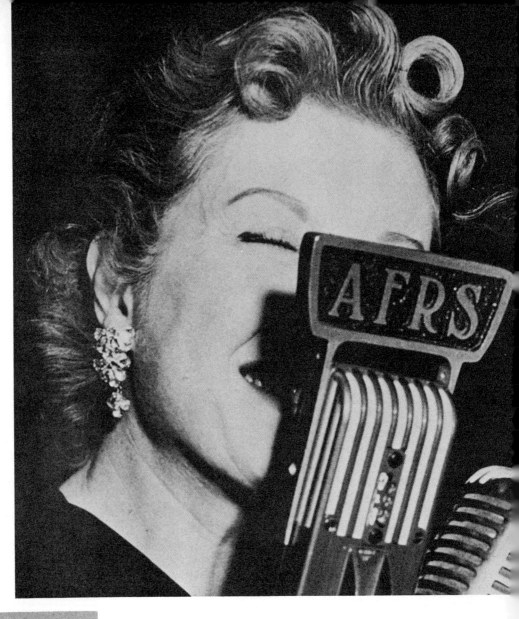

Greer

MIKE FRIGHT

Dottie

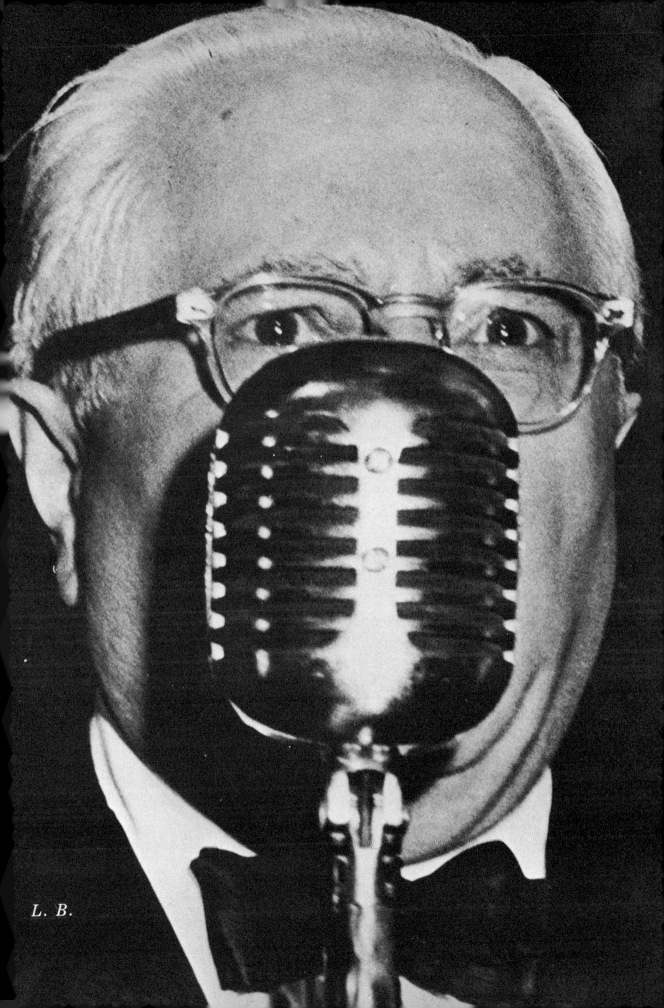

L. B.

Louella—the elusive exclusive

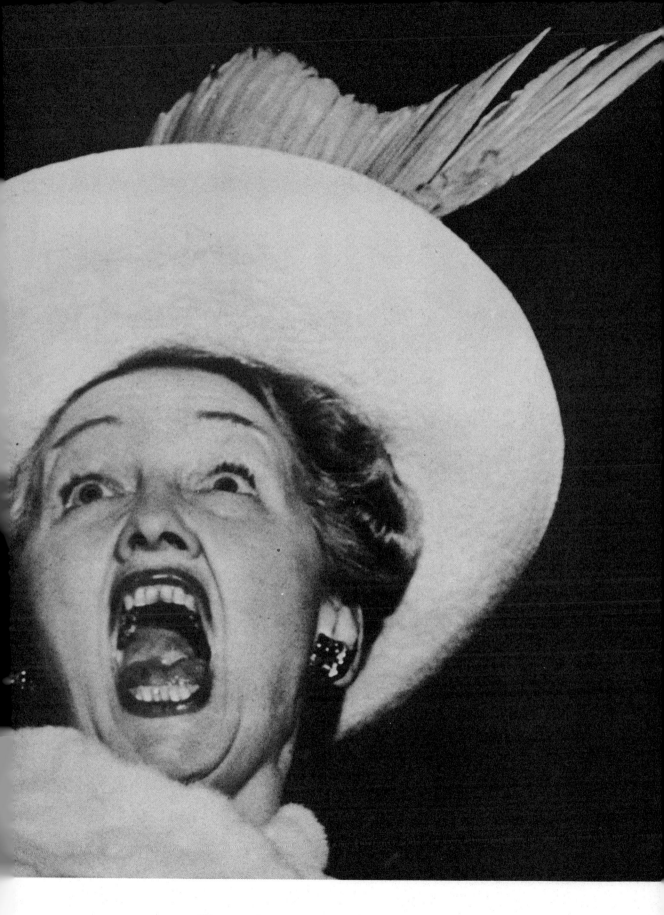

. . . Hopper's topper

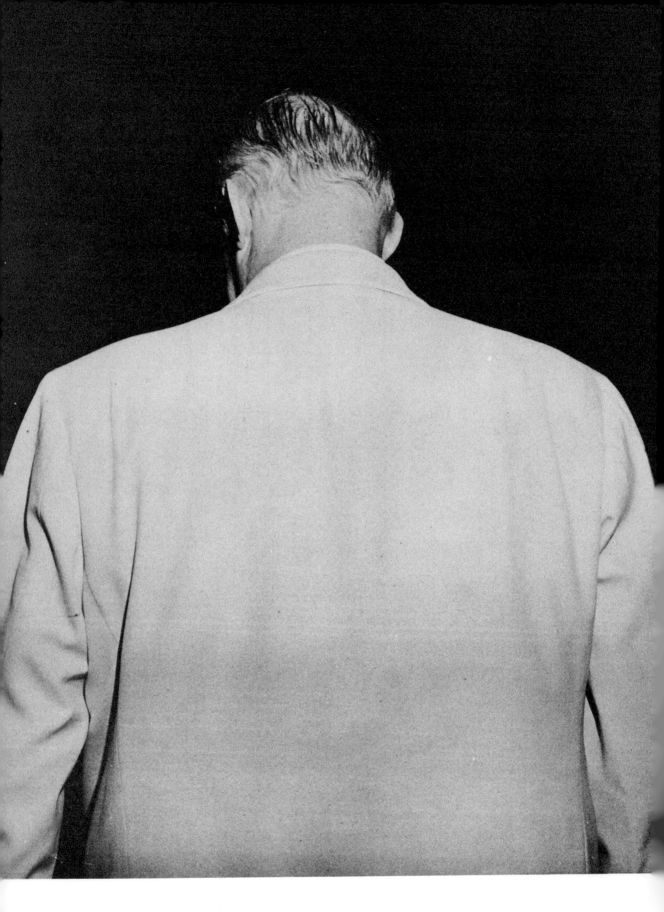

Sidney

Oscar

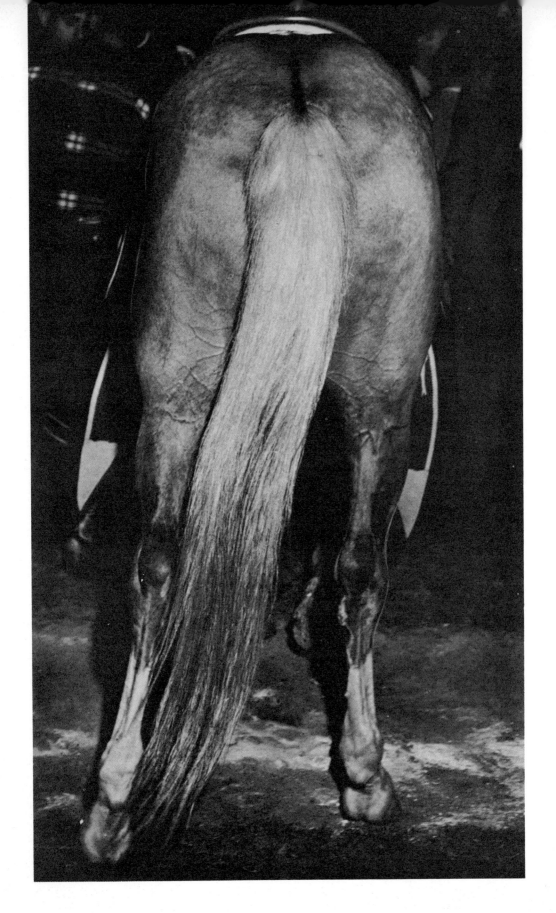

Trigger

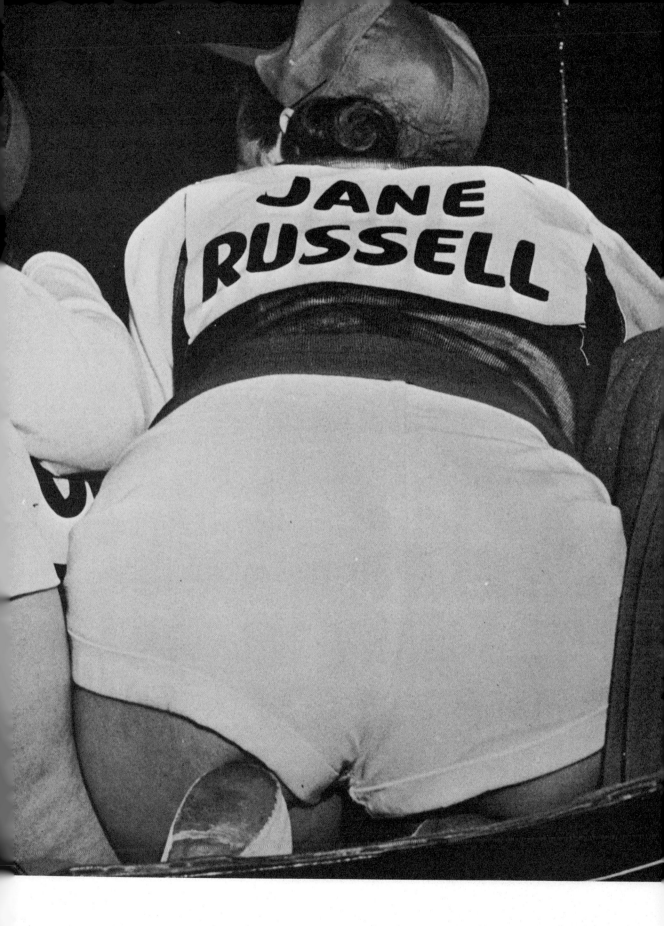

H. Fonda and friend

C. Farrell and friend

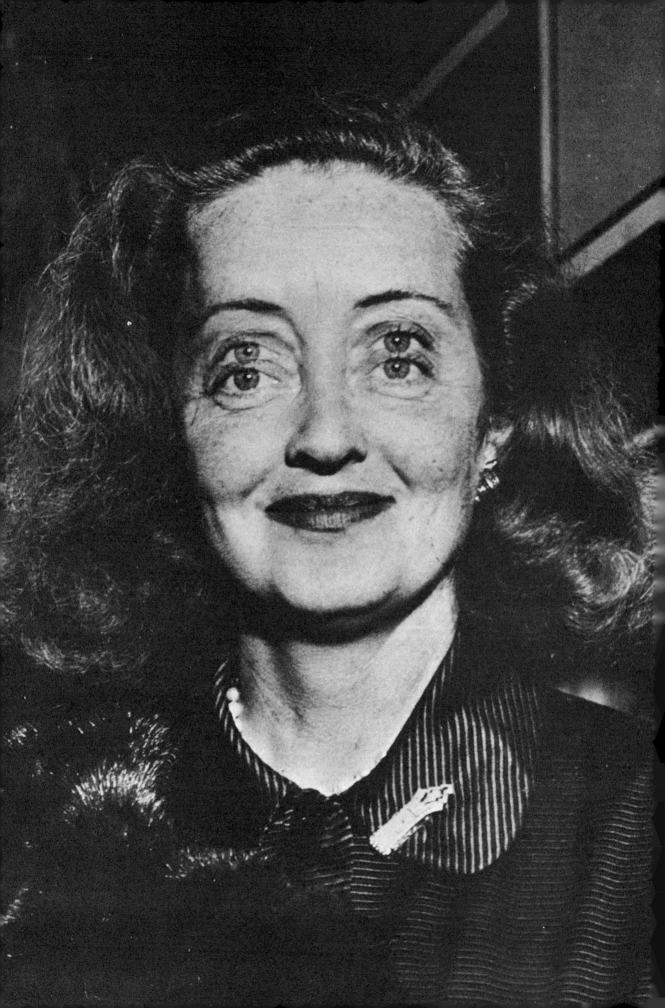

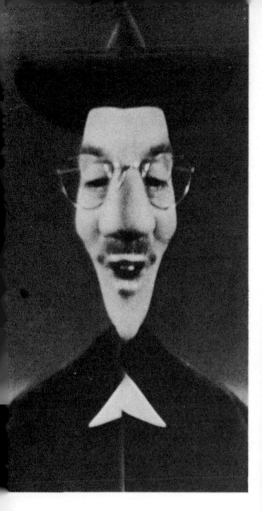

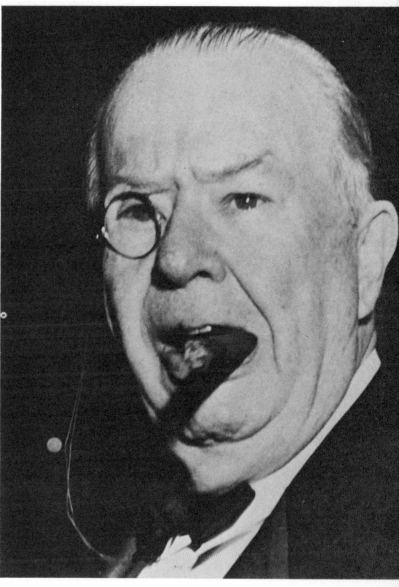

PUPILS OF THE DRAMA

Combined age — thirty-nine

VETERANS

America's Sweetheart and buddy

Introvert

Extrovert

CASTING
OFFICE
←

Ready . . .

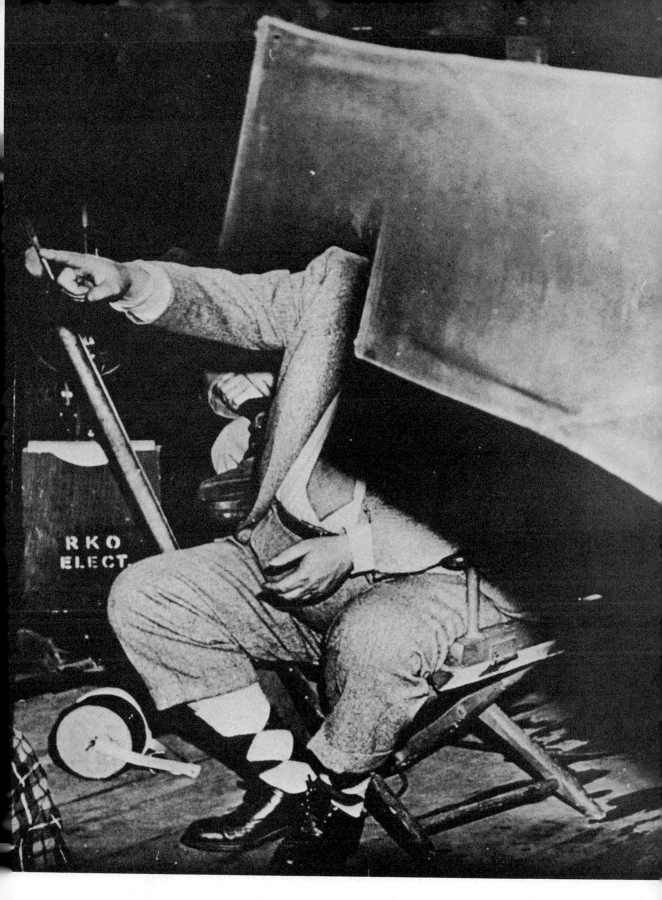

"...include me out!"

PARAMOUNT - "WHEN WORLDS COLLIDE"

FILM EDITING		"A PLACE IN THE SUN" - WM. HORNBECK
DOCUMENTARY	SHORT	"BENJY" - FRED ZINNEMANN - PAR.
	FEATURE	"KON-TIKI" - ARTFILM, RKO RADIO
COSTUME DESIGN	B&W	"A PLACE IN THE SUN" - EDITH HEAD
	COLOR	"AN AMERICAN IN PARIS"
SCIENTIFIC or TECHNICAL	3 CLASS 2 AWARDS - PARAMOUNT - JENNINGS STANCLIFFE	
		-MGM OLIN DUPY
		-RCA VICTOR
ART DIRECTION	B&W - "A STREETCAR NAMED DESIRE" R. DAY	
	COLOR - "AN AMERICAN IN PARIS" - GIBBONS & CARFAGNO	
SET DECORATION	B&W - "A STREETCAR NAMED DESIRE" - HOPKINS	
	COLOR - "AN AMERICAN IN PARIS" - WILLIS & GLEASON	
SHORT SUBJECTS	CARTOON	"TWO MOUSEKETEERS" - FRED QUIMBY
	ONE REEL	"WORLD OF KIDS" - ROBERT YOUNGSON
	TWO REEL	"NATURE'S HALF ACRE" - WALT DISNEY
SOUND RECORDING	"THE GREAT CARUSO" - DOUGLAS SHEARER MGM	
CINEMATOGRAPHY	B&W - "A PLACE IN THE SUN" WILLIAM C. MELLOR	
"	COLOR - "AN AMERICAN IN PARIS" ALFRED GILKS & JOHN ALTON	
SPECIAL AWARDS	GENE KELLY	
	IRVING THALBERG - MR. ARTHUR FREED	
FOREIGN LANGUAGE	"RASHOMON"	
MUSIC	BEST SONG	"IN THE COOL, COOL, COOL OF THE EVENING" HOAGY CARMICHAEL & JOHNNY MERCER
	SCORE MUSICAL PICTURE	"AN AMERICAN IN PARIS" GREEN CHAPLIN
	" DRAMA OR COMEDY	"A PLACE IN THE SUN" - WAXMAN
WRITING	MOT. PIC. STORY	"SEVEN DAYS TO NOON" DEHN & BERNARD
	SCREEN PLAY	"A PLACE IN THE SUN" - PAR. MICHAEL WILSON & HARRY BROWN
	STORY & SCREEN PLAY	"AN AMERICAN IN PARIS" ALAN JAY LERNER
DIRECTION	"A PLACE IN THE SUN" - PARA. GEORGE STEVENS	
SUPPORT. ACTOR		
" **ACTRESS**		
BEST ACTOR		
BEST ACTRESS		
PICTURE		

Score board

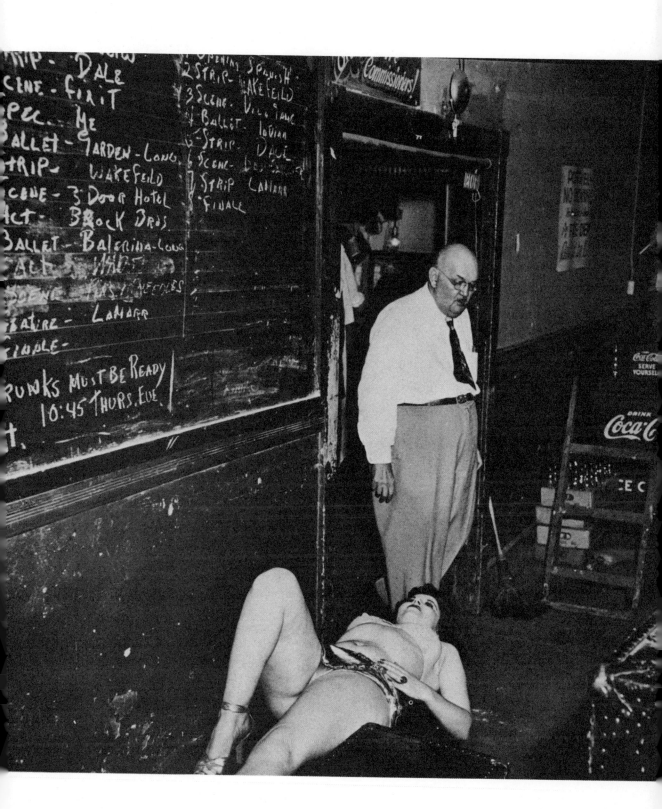

Call board

Animal "Osca

FILMS' TIGHTENED PURSESTRINGS

OVERHAULING AT ALL COS.

Film industry in a large measure is adopting still another austerity program. In addition to a further tightening of pursestrings on production budgets, some distrib toppers are now demanding new economies ranging from a wholesale lopping of expense accounts to cutting of salaries on the exec level and elimination of personnel.

Notice has been posted at the Paramount homeoffice that expense vouchers covering items other than those which are absolutely necessary will be disallowed. Spyros P. Skouras, president of 20th, is on the record with a promise to stockholders that substantial new savings in overhead will be effected this year. He said that the employment of some persons will be terminated and some salaries . . . to important . . . , will be . . .

. . . portedly de- . . . of its three . . . its at the . . . bout 27 per- . . . have been . . . roll as much . . . in the con- . . . as shifted to

. . . fice space . . . may be cut . . . ent economy . . . brass is ex- . . . t the studi . . . the possibil . . . pix at lesse . . . yeing its th . . . the aim of sa . . . WB plan is . . . of its vario . . . g one field . . . work of oth . . . nnel at the

. . . company he . . . rying about . . . expenditure . . . isses out a . . . is abnorm . . . im, presider . . . ut it this

"We're startled by how high . . . ness can go and startled by . . . low it can be. The former . . . daries at which business le . . . off seem to have disappeared . . . The new economies are, . . . fect, designed as at least a . . . cushion to ease the blow . . . heavy losses with the sh . . . standard pix. In any eve . . .

Hollywood Collateral Loan Association

1612 NORTH VINE ST. • HEmpstead 6490

CALIFORNIA COLLATERAL LOAN BROKERS ASSOCIATION MEMBER

Nº 1207

Hollywood 28, Calif.

DEC 21 195

19

$ 3

I hereby pledge to HOLLYWOOD COLLATERAL LOAN ASSOCIATION, the following described property, to-wit:

One Ring

Three

DOLLARS,

to secure payment of a loan in the sum of _____ (the receipt of which is hereby acknowledged) together with interest and charges as herein provided. It is agreed that said loan shall bear interest and/or other charges from date until paid at the maximum rate permitted by the statutes of California, as provided by Section 2, Chapter 538 of the Statutes of 1935, as amended by the Statutes of 1939, Chapter 951, but that I shall not be personally liable for the repayment of said loan, interest or other charges and that pledgee shall have recourse to the pledged property only for the payment thereof. It is further agreed that the last day for redemption of this pledge shall be thirty (30) days after the date hereof. Payment or acceptance of interest after maturity date shall not extend the redemption date unless such extension is endorsed on the reverse side hereof. In the event of default I expressly waive demand of performance and the giving of notice of time and place of sale and agree that said property may be sold at either public or private sale and that pledgee may be a purchaser if the property is sold at public sale. Pledgee shall not be liable for loss or damage to the pledged property arising from fire, theft, robbery, burglary, Act of God or the Public enemy, or in any event for more than 25%, in addition to the principal amount of the loan. Pledgee may at its option pay any liens or charges due or becoming due upon or against the pledged property and the amount paid shall be added to the loan secured hereby. I agree that all payments of interest and principal must be made at the office of the pledgee, I hereby authorize the pledgee to deliver the pledged property to the bearer of the duplicate copy of pledge agreement whether or not endorsed by me and agree that such delivery shall release pledgee from further liability and that the duplicate copy shall constitute a receipt for the pledged property. I represent that I am the owner of said property, that it is free and clear of encumbrances, and that I am authorized to pledge the same.

HOLLYWOOD COLLATERAL LOAN ASSOCIATION is hereby authorized to deliver to bearer the above described pledged property. Any loan of $100.00 and over requires 24 hours notice for redemption.

The laws of the State of California provide as follows: Section 3 of Chapter 538 Statutes of 1935 as amended by Chapter 951, Statutes of 1939.

"Every pawn-broker shall retain in his possession every article pledged to him for a period of . . .

Dated: _____ 19____

SIX MONTHS after the last date fixed for redemption by his loan contract."

MUST HAVE ORIGINAL SIGNATURE TO REDEEM

SIGN HERE ☞

Signed _____

MINIMUM CHARGE 50c PER MONTH

INTEREST PAYABLE MONTHLY

Pix biz nix

What am I bid?

CATALOGUE

FRENCH PROVINCIAL   XVIII CENTURY ENGLISH

AND OTHER FURNITURE

EMERSON TELEVISION   CAPEHART COMBINATION

STEINWAY GRAND PIANO

FABULOUS COLLECTION OF

DIAMOND AND PRECIOUS STONE JEWELRY

FRENCH AND AMERICAN MODERN OIL PAINTINGS

BY WORLD FAMOUS ARTISTS

FINE LIBRARY AND LARGE RECORD COLLECTION

EUROPEAN PORCELAINS   CRYSTAL CHANDELIERS

SILVER — BRASS — COPPER — PEWTER

and

THE ENTIRE PERSONAL WARDROBE INCLUDING

MINK AND OTHER FINE FURS

REMOVED FROM THE BEVERLY HILLS MANSION OF

MISS HEDY LAMARR

Together with Important Consignments
From Other Owners

PUBLIC AUCTION

PART I

Beginning Monday, June 25, 1951

PART II

Beginning Monday, July 2, 1951

PART III

Sunday, July 9, Afternoon and Evening

ARTHUR B. GOODE

LOUIS E. WASS   AUCTIONEERS

8470 W   5197

WEbster 5197

Hedy slept here

Miss Hedy Lamarr's spacious mansion on No. Roxbury Drive,
Beverly Hills.

Objet d'art

Art lovers

Zsa Zsa

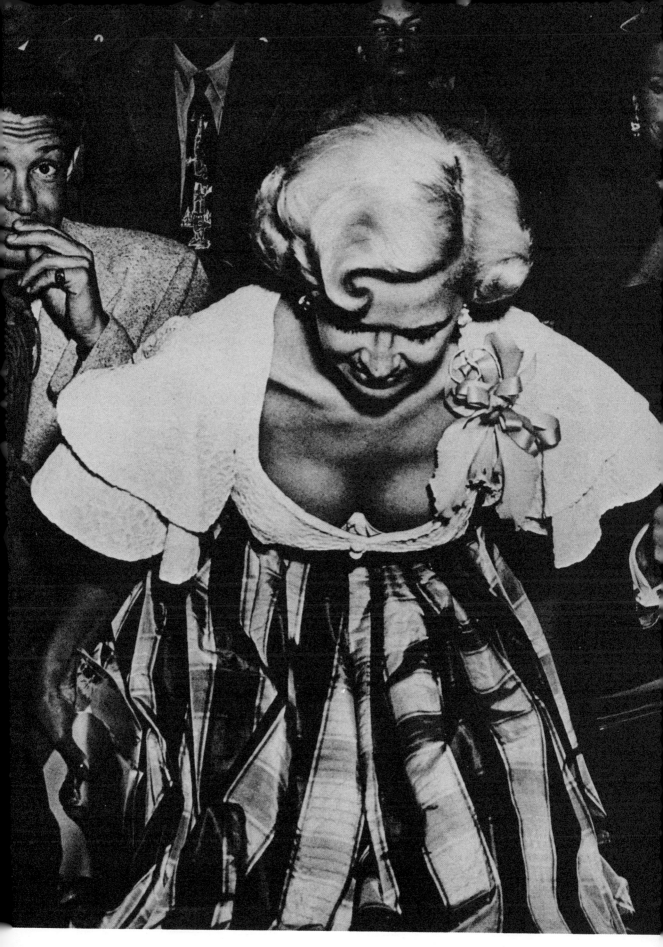

Marilyn

the Mason

"...A Jug of Wine, A Loaf of Bread..."

Liz

od Ladd

the Dean

olonic Irrigation

n Paula S 310 N Soto.........ANgls 7010
 Wolf 1916 S Westrn..........REpblc 3-2804

RALAVAGE INSTITUTE
Altralavage Cleanses Not Only the Colon,
But Also the 22 Feet of Small Intestines
Where Foods Absorb - Dr. L. G. Zaboy, D.C.
346 S Spring...............MUtul 6972

assador Lido Health Club
    Ambassadr Hotel.DUnkrk 9-1336

ERICAN HEALTH ASSN INC
    1237 S Fairfx.WEbstr 3-2771

DREASEN CARL R 4100 Bevrly.DUnkrk 9-6346
les Massage & Therapeutic Clinic
    2200 S Sn Pedro.PRspct 4611

ER-HOLTH LEIF
LATEST IN COLONICS
PHYSIO-THERAPY - MEN & WOMEN
BIO-ENGINEERING & NUTRITION
6757 Sunset Bl...............HIlsde 9463

berry Health Rendezvous 8009 Melrse.YOrk 6080
gley B F 1178 W Adms.............RIchmd 1520

RSAM & BARSAM
DR VIOLET E. BARSAM, D.C.
DR BENJAMIN BARSAM, D.C.
Colon Irrigation - Dierker System
7209 S Vermont Av..........PLsnt 1-7221

TTLE CREEK HEALTH SERVICE
    345 S Hill.MIchgn 8384
tle Creek Methods Office
    5648 Hollywd.GRnit 3233

TTLE CREEK WILSHIRE
COLON IRRIGATIONS
DIERKER SYSTEM
Treatments for Colitis - Constipation
Colds - Flu - Arthritis - Neuritis - Sciatica
Fever Therapy

3866 W 6th.............DUnkrk 9-3016
    Near Western Ave

nda Margaret Maney
    1619 W Olympc.DUnkrk 7-0360
tmore Health Club 515 S Olive...MIchgn 1011
ck A B 8344 Melrse..........WYomng 7742
nchart John B 7170½ Melrse....WHitny 4588
del G L
Dierker System
3718 W Pico...............REpblc 3-5770

MHNET R H
Corner of Florence & Vermont
7129 S Vermnt...............PLsnt 1-2387

WLBY CECIL DR & STAFF
EMERGENCY COLONICS
Day & Night - Eves. - Sat. - Sun. & Holidays
SINCE 1933 - NEAR VENICE BLVD.
1504 S Vermont..........DUnkrk 7-3706

OOKS L A
SOUTHWEST DISTRICT
PAINLESS - PLEASANT - HEALTHFUL
LADY ATTENDANT FOR WOMEN
1310 W Sta Barbara Av....AXmnstr 2-2229

URGESS H T

BEVERLY AT VERMONT
Dr. H. T. Burgess, D.C.
DIERKER COLONICS
NURSE IN ATTENDANCE
Dietetics - X-Ray
Electrotherapy
SPECIAL ATTENTION TO DISEASES
OF THE RECTUM EXCEPT CANCER

3803 Beverly Bl.............OLmpia 8064
If no ans call................NOrmndy 2-5535

ALIF HEALTH SERVICE
    248 S Oxfrd.DUnkrk 8-4725
rroll Paul M 8627 S Vermnt........TWnoks 5084
hiropractic Health Service
    4511 S Avaln.CEntry 2-7621
lark J Walter 7518 Calif Av HtgPrk.LAfayet 7032
oghlan Harry W 4857 Bevrly.......GLdstn 0788
olonics Steam Bath & Massage
    5810 N Figroa.CLevld 7-1380
opelin Saml C 634 S Westrn......DUnkrk 8-3667

COTNER JENNIE S

Corrective Health Service
10 YEARS IN
Wilshire-Western Area

Jennie S. Cotner, D.C. & Staff

FOR
MEN & WOMEN
DIERKER COLONIC SYSTEM
Massage - Baths & Physical Therapy

3808 Ingraham............DUnkrk 9-4088

Creech Clyde C 7525 S Vermnt......TWnoks 7823
Cregger F 2528 W Sta Barb Av....AXmnstr 1-0033
CRENSHAW PROFESSIONAL GROUP
    Dierker $3.50
    942 Crenshw............WEbstr 6128
Dailey Donald J 714 W Vernon.........ADms 8378
Dailey's Health Institute 714 W Vernon..ADms 8378
DAY CELETE 249 N Vermnt.......DUnkrk 9-3933
    Dunn Florence
    Hours 9 to 4 Evenings & Sat by Appt
    5149 York.............CLevld 6-7374
Eames Isabelle T 8580 Melrse Av.....CRstvw 5-0318

ERICSON'S
IN HOLLYWOOD
SEPARATE MEN'S & WOMEN'S DEPTS.
1769 Cahuenga........HOlywd 9-1991
2 Blks. W. of Vine - 1 Blk. N. of Hollywood Bl.

ERNST HOWARD W
TOX - ELIMINATOR
Latest and Most Scientific Colon Therapy
BEVERLY AND WESTERN
247 N Western Av...........GLdstn 1103

Ernst Howard W 247 N Westn.......GLdstn 1103
Forder Wm T 4507 S Figroa.......AD ms-7679
Frazier Hortense 7701½ S Figroa....THrnwal 0685
Goodfellow Sidney J 1112 W Flornce..TWnoks 3991
GRIFFITTS JAS R
Colonic Irrigations Given in the Home
6534½ Whittr................ANgls 3-4455
GROSSMAN HARRY
OIL COLONICS
Using Antiseptic Oil Solutions
The Clinical Proven Treatment for Colitis
Constipation & Resulting Diseases
All Treatments Include Physio Therapy
LADY TECHNICIAN - X-RAY ON PREMISES
2 Blks. West of Alvarado - Free Parking
2245 W 8th...............DUnkrk 7-1781

Grossman Harry 2245 W 8th.......DUnkrk 7-1781
Hollywd Ericson's 1769 Cahuenga...HOlywd 9-1991
HOLLYWOOD MINERAL BATHS
    5625 Melrse Av.GLdstn 2149
    If no ans call................HIlsde 7336

HOLMES RALPH FREDRICK
21 YEARS SAME LOCATION
WILSHIRE & VERMONT DIST
COLONIC IRRIGATIONS
DIERKER SYSTEM
Colitis, Rheumatism
Arthritis - Neuritis - Colds
Piles, Prostate Treatments
LADIES' AND MEN'S DEPARTMENTS
684 S Vermont Av...........DUnkrk 3-9327

Holmes Ralph Fredrick
    684 S Vermnt Av.DUnkrk 3-9327
Hotchkiss Carl 5648 Hollywd Bl.......GRnit 3233

Sell through the Yellow Pages.

SIXTH AND BROADWAY
DOWNTOWN DISTRICT
Dr. Van W. McElwain, D.C.
DRUGLESS THERAPY
Specialist in the Field of
COLONICS
Liver & Gallbladder Therapy
X-Ray Diagnosis - Radionics
NURSE IN ATTENDANCE

VAndike 9718

610 SOUTH BROADWAY - SUITE 909

Hotkins Mark E 8463½ S Vermnt...THrnwal 0854
Howling Gordon 2703 Walnt WalPrk...LOgan 5-6546
HUDSON BEATRICE N
TOX-ELIMINATOR
LATEST SCIENTIFIC COLON THERAPY
Treatments & Dietetics - Graduate Nurse
8412 S Main...............TWnoks 2448

Hudson Beatrice N 8412 S Main......TWnoks 2448
HUNT TERRY HEALTH SYSTEM
    50 ½ La Cienega Bl.CRstvw 6-9131
Johanna's Health Studio
    314 S Rampt.DUnkrk 4-8033
JOHNSON ARTHUR LEE
    4707 Crenshw.AXmnstr 6312
Johnson's Bath House 2715 S Westrn..PArkwy 0393
JONES ORA M

GRADUATE COLON THERAPIST
KENNISON HYDRO TONE
Most Scientific Method for
COLON IRRIGATION

FREE CONSULTATION

RES. - DUnkirk 9-9760

5209 S Broadway...........ADms 3-4802

Joyce Clyde J 1122 W Sta Barb...AXmnstr 7-3617
Kammerer & Kammerer
    3514 Eagle Rk Bl.ALbny 2218
KENT PETER S 579 N Larchmnt.....GLdstn 6225
Keyse System 4668 Hollywd.......NOrmndy 2-8861
KING A THOS
See Our Ad under Chiropractors
    4365 Avain.............ADms 1-2274
Klein Zamvill
Helium Oxygen for Intestinal Conditions
    960 N Westrn...........HEmstd 8585
LEVIN MIRIAM 5717½ S Fairfx.......YOrk 5371
LINDEN JOSEPH P 1330 W 6th...DUnkrk 7-8241
Linna Reed Slenderizing Salons
    3254 Wilshr.DUnkrk 4-1760
LOOMIS DONALD ANTHONY
    6433 Crenshw.PLsnt 2-3743
L A COLLEGE OF MASSAGE &
PHYSIO-THERAPY
FACE AND BODY CONTOURING
COLONIC - BATHS - MASSAGE
3808 Ingraham............DUnkrk 3-8223
LUCARELL JAS M
See Our Ad under Chiropractors
    205 S Westrn...........DUnkrk 3-0143
Mackintosh Alice D 6302 York......ALbny 4257
McCormick A
Results Absolutely Without Drugs
    638 W 40th Pl..........CEntry 2-9476
McCoy Lester M 448 W 3rd......WEbstr 3-8863
McELWAIN VAN W
DOWNTOWN DISTRICT
X-Ray & COLONIC Specialist
NURSE IN ATTENDANCE
610 S Broadway...........VAndk 9718

McElwain Van W 610 S Bdway......VAndk 9718
    (See Advertisement This Page)
MERRITT L J
See Display Ad under Chiropractors
    219 W 7th...............VAndk 4246
Millnizer R B 3676 Whittr Bl........AN gls-5975
Miyaoka Frank Y 258 E 1st..........MUtul 5419
Moody Vernice 1134 E 23rd.........RIchmd 9752
MOORE HERBERT R 2708 W 48th.AXmnstr 1-0953
Mullniks C W 7130 Rugby Av HtgPk...KImbl 4796
Neely Loyd E 610 S Bdway...........VAndk 4285
New Yorker Technique 355 S Bdway...TRnity 7031

Nier Henry V 707 S Bdway............DU
Papa Alice 745 S Alvarado............DU
PERRIN C C DR SCIENTIFIC HEALTH
INSTITUTE
Huntington Park-Southeast Area
    7904 Pacific HtgPrk...........JEfrsn
Reed Herbert W 2e24 W 6th.........DUnkrk 3-92
Reed Linna Slenderizing Salons
    3254 Wilshr.DUnkrk 4-17
Robinson Chas C 871 E Vernon.......ADms 1-
SANDERS KEITH F
Gastro-Intestinal Disorders
    1512 Hillhrst Av..........OLmpia 9-
Saunders Bernard 1759 E 102nd......LOgan 7-
Schmiedel R A
Dierker Colonics-Nurse Attending
    6051 Melrse.............GRnit 3-
Seibold Marty 308 N Heliotrope Dr..NOrmndy 1-2
SHRADER ALVIN A & TED L
    5260 S Figroa.CEntry 2-5
Simpson Institute of Physical Culture
Dierker Method Relieves Constipator
    3417 Whittr Bl...........ANgls 1-3
Skold Colonic Irrination 101 N Larchmnt.GLd
SPURR HAROLD A 4867 Eagle Rk Bl..ALbny
Stock R Jeane 407 W 6th.............NOrmndy 2-2
Stockton Wallace G 7125 W 6th.......DUnkrk 4-8
SULTAN TURKISH BATHS INC
    607 S Hill.VAndk 3
    (See Advertisement This Page)
Swedish Institute
Dierker Colonic Treatment
    1820 W 9th..............DUnkrk 9-5
TAYLOR A H 5654 Hollywd.........GRnit 3
Tyler Tamzon 745 S Kern Av.........ANgls 1-2
URBACH IRVIN B
$2 Colonic-Nurse in Attendance
    604 S Rampt.............DUnkrk 7-
VALDOVINOS G D 2109 Whittr........ANgls
Vigil Toby 8535 Hollywd............ALbny
Vroom Iva A 4509 S Hoovr...........CEntry 2-
WILLIAMS AL HEALTH SYSTEMS
COLONICS - DIERKER SYSTEM
ESTABLISHED SINCE 1920
727 W 7th...............TRnity 29

Wilshire Battle Creek 3866 W 6th..DUnkrk 9-
WILSHIRE WOMEN'S HEALTH CLUB
    5364 Wilshr.WEbstr

Colonic Therapy Apparatu
& Supplies

Ace Detoxinator Co 654 S Westlke..DUnkrk 4-
CUTLER PHYSICIANS' EQUIPMENT CO
See Ad under Phys & Surgs Equip & Supplies
    926 Venice..............PRspct
Fimmen E M 8516 Walnut Dr..........GLdst
Lindquist R J & Co 2419 W 9th......DUnkrk 2
Mason Distributors 5071 W Washn......YOrk
National Medical Products Co
    7620 S Centrl.LOgan 5
New Yorker Clinic 355 S Bdway.......TRnity
PHYSICAL THERAPY CO
    3330 W 6th.DUnkrk 7
ROYCE PRODUCTS
NATIONAL MEDICAL PRODUCTS CO
    7620 S Centrl.LOgan 5
TOX ELIMINATOR MFG CO
    919 E Doran Gln.CHapmn

Learn who sells things or who
pairs things by referring to
Yellow Pages. They are pac
with useful information.

. A. Directory

uyers. More and more people
"Look inside the Classified" before
buying.

Colonics—nature spelled backwards

ERKER COLONICS

PARKING IN REAR

PATIEN

HANGMAN'S
TREE LOUSY
FOOD

WARM
BEER

+

EMERGENCY
HOSPITAL
RESTAURANT
HOME COOKED
~ MEALS ~
STEAKS CHOPS

HOT BEER
LOUSY FOOD

Francis dances

To Mickey add ⅓ Ritz

Another Hollywood turkey

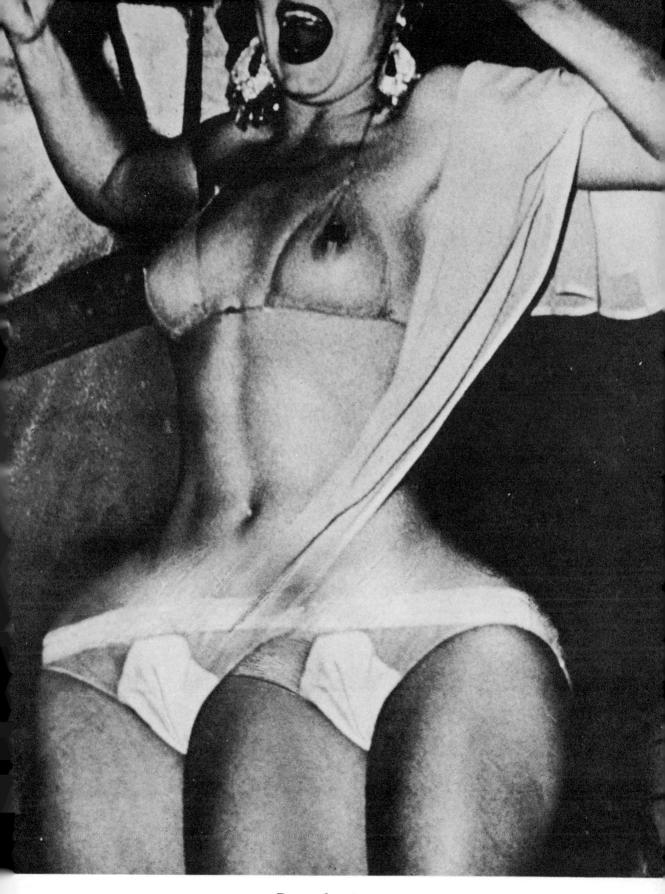

Busy hostess

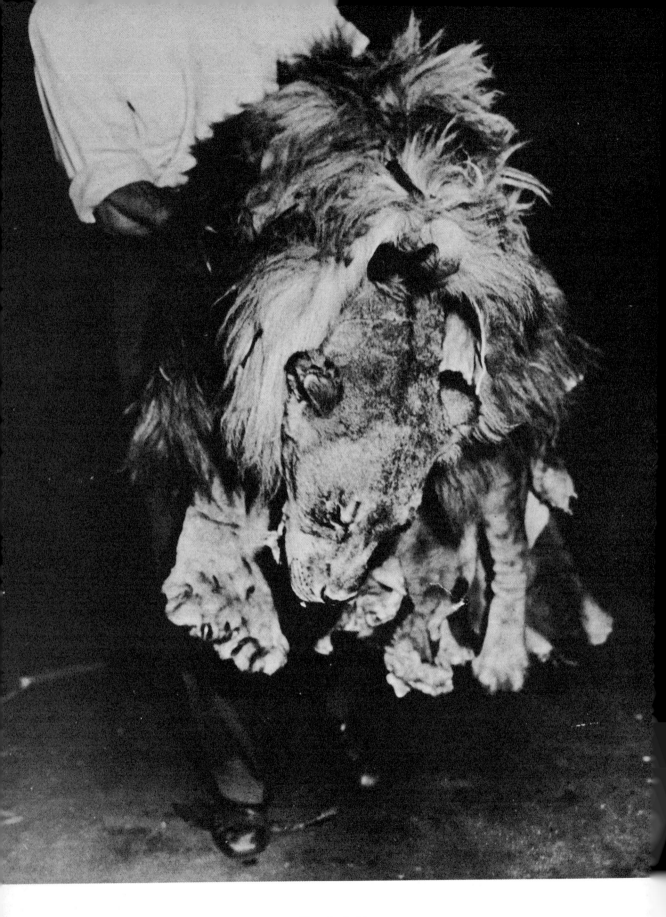

Social lion

Morning after

ODDLY ENOUGH, a close proximity to the Dream Factories has had small effect on Hollywood itself.

Except for a rather weird approach to the merchandising of food and death, a sprinkling of assorted characters and a few architectural monstrosities, it differs little from other communities.

As elsewhere, the people pursue the dollar, with which to buy happiness. As elsewhere, they thrill to parades, live stars and the patter of little feet.

HOLLYWOOD BLVD. VINE ST.

6290

...AND ALICE
EVERY SUN
EVENING ON
KFI 5:30

LUNCHEO
NOW BEING SER

Rexall

Act IV   STREET SCENE

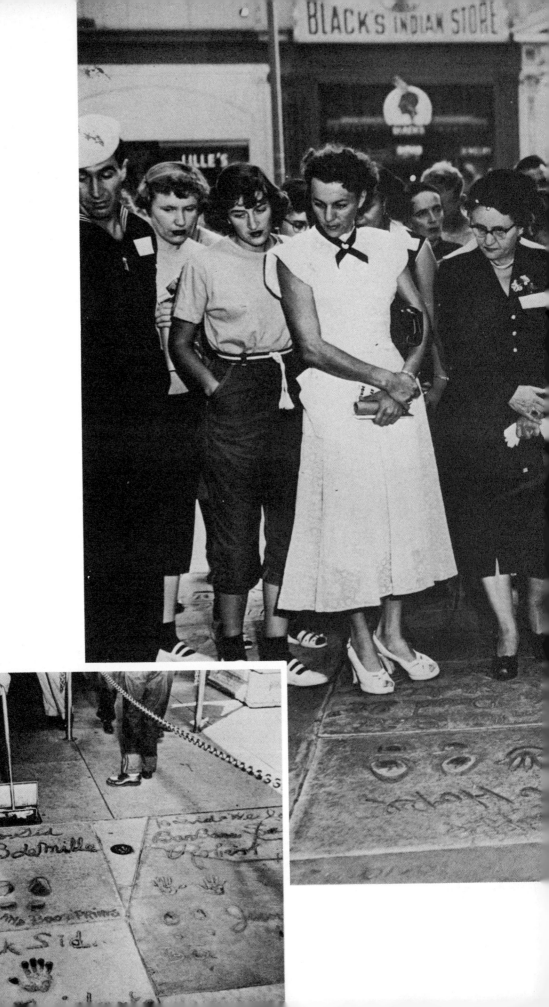

t prints in the sands of Grauman's

MIRACLE ON HOLLYWOOD BLVD

Hot house Santa

Synthetic angel

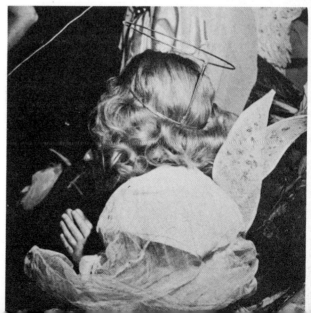

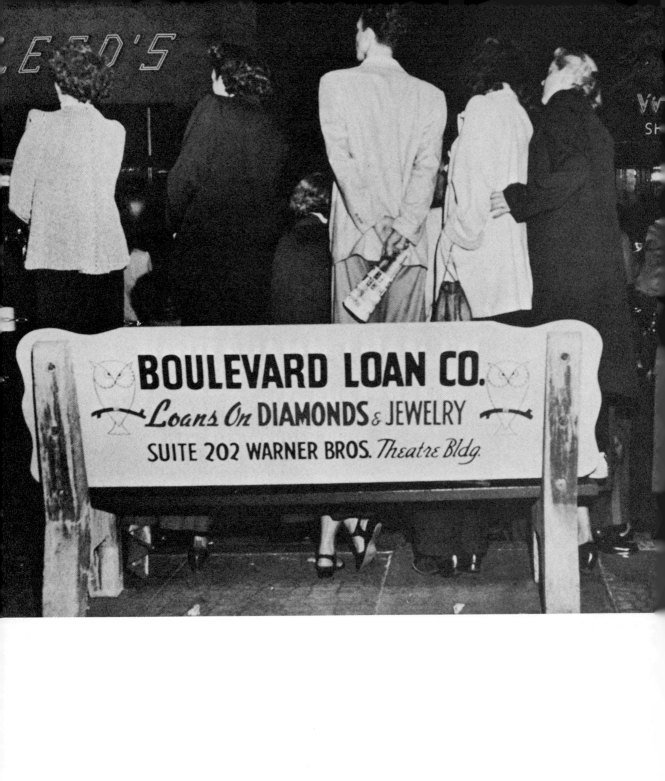

IT PAYS TO ADVERTISE

If I had a million

Quo Vadis

The Asphalt Jungle

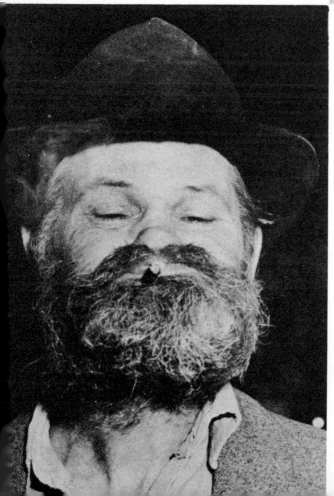

Hey, Figaro!

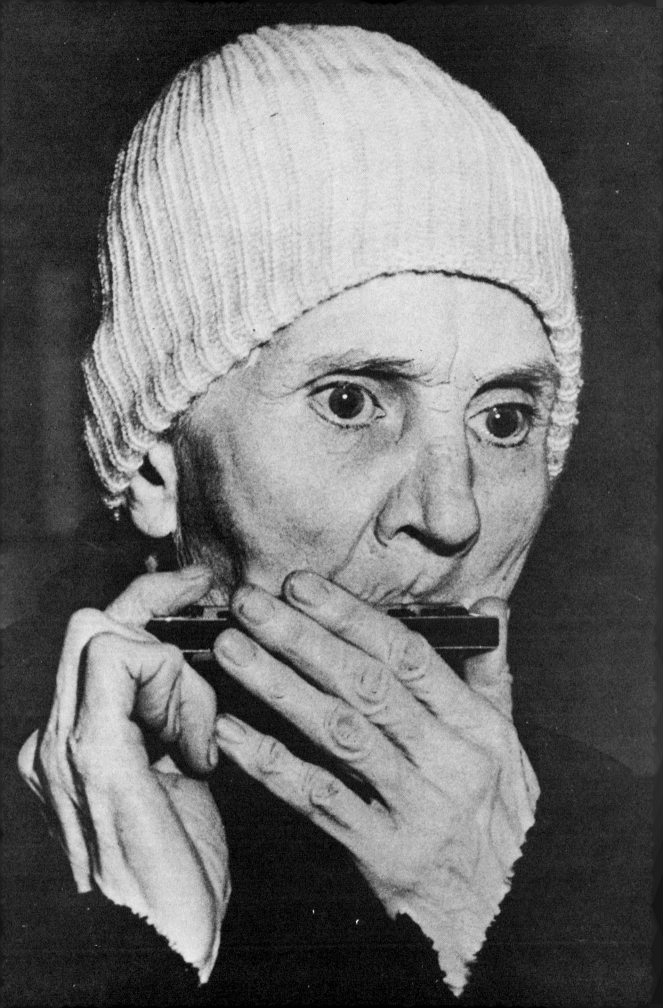

ITH A SONG IN MY HEART

Park and see

TOGETHER THE GREATEST HORROR SHOW OF ALL TIME !

SCREAMY   WEIRD   HORRIFIC

CHILLING

FRANK   EIN

Movies are better than ever

THE END?

The authors would like to point out that
NAKED HOLLYWOOD was produced with the
aid and assistance of a Speed Graphic camera,
Wollensak lenses, Westinghouse flash bulbs, an
Omega enlarger, Designers 3, Bettman Archives
and — Hollywood, California.